unapologetically ANOIN†ED

JERRIKA LEAKES

Jerrika Leakes

Illustrations by Joshua Smith and Patricia McBride
Editing and Formatting by Teresa Janes

Unless otherwise indicated, all Scripture references are taken from the New King James Version on BibleGateway.com.

Dedication

I dedicate this book to my late Grandma Verlean White who was a great inspiration in my life. During the many conversations we would have over breakfast they always included God. You taught me that if I keep God at the center of all I do, I can never go wrong. It was this very principle and sound of your voice that inspired me to write this book.

Acknowledgments

I want to take this time to acknowledge the people who have been instrumental in assisting me with the creation of this book and in life. To my Pastors, Ronnie and Jacquetta Cole, thank you for being my gateway to restoration. To my prayer circle who always have my back... Ms. Dora, Quita, Shavetta, Shard, Junia, Dorian, and my church True Revival and Praise.

To all my siblings, Jemia, Jon, Jerry, Tanya, Dwaun, Trell, and Johnice, thank you for believing in me. I am so proud of all of you. The things you are doing in life push me to be better. It is a blessing to have the bond that we have.

Dad, thank you for believing in me. You have always supported me in all that I do. You never speak anything negative, always the positive. Mama, thank you for being a light. You are such an encourager.

To my boys, Darion and Kell, I love you with everything in me. You keep me going. Thank you for making it easy to be your mom. I also appreciate the constructive criticism you give to keep me 100...lol.

Special thanks to April Hudson for book cover design as well as Joshua Smith, and Patricia McBride for the illustrations. All of you have creative and gifted hands. The images you put together brought the chapters in the book to life. Photographer Candance Moore, you are the best at capturing the look! I look fiyah on the cover. Thank you for marketing and web design, Keedra Smith.

To my editor Teresa Janes, all I can say is everyone needs a Teresa on their team. You made this process smooth. Thanks, birthday sister! (Insider)

To my friends, Pastor Samantha Westbrook, Felisha Cobbs and Erica Hart, thank you for being so genuine and open. I appreciate you for giving me direction, advice, and insight on how to write a book.

To my favorite lady in the entire world, my beautiful mom, Arlene Hicks. Thank you for your constant push and encouragement to keep going. You are the true definition of a "Proverbs 31 woman." The core values you instilled in me have been so beneficial in my life and I will treasure them forever. Also, thanks Pop (Dwight Hicks) for always giving me sound advice and support.

Last but certainly not least...To my husband, Demario Leakes. I could write a book on you alone about how you love me without limits. Thank you for being my biggest fan and covering. You are the best man, best dad, supporter, financer, and friend! I thank Donna Herron and Reginald Leakes for getting together and creating you.

Jerrika Leakes

Contents

Chapter One

Is there anyone like me?

Okay, no need for an introduction. This is the introduction! If you have picked up this book, preferably bought or been blessed with, then there are some things we need to clear the air on first. Let's touch on all checkpoints:

Is there anyone like me? You grew up during a time when music was your mentor and seemed to be the way you healed from hurt.

Is there anyone like me? You grew up during a time when living in silos was a thing of the past? If there was a party on Friday night, it didn't matter who threw it you were there, PERIODT.

Is there anyone like me, who sees all people as beautiful, holding their own unique treasure, and always excited to meet them wherever you go?

Is there anyone like me that knows you are anointed, but also got swag? You wouldn't be you if you didn't stay dripped for Jesus.

Is there anyone like me, who loves to praise God, but is also not ashamed to hit the dance floor and join the line for the line dance?

Is there anyone like me, who loves a good worship song, but also loves to bump a good rap song (clean version/if it's saying something motivating), and is not afraid to bump it loud while listening?

Is there anyone like me, who will pray for any and everyone, but also is not afraid to slap cards, play dominos, and talk smack while playing volleyball at the family reunion?

Yeah I know...for some this may be too much, but for those who catch my vibe keep reading cause this book is for you.

I grew up in the church. Every Sunday my mother woke us up for church. It was a struggle for me sometimes to get up, but once I got there it was okay. I loved to hear the word, loved to be in the place of worship, loved to sing in the choir, and overall just downright loved God. The only question I battled with, was did GOD truly love me? You would think going to church every Sunday, there is no way one could feel like this, but that's the thing. In research over the years and talking with others, I have found that many also grew up in church but still missing that divine relationship and encounter with God. I got to a point where church had become predictable and routine.

Thinking back, I remember singing in the choir and when it was time to get the word, I would find a reason to ease out because I knew it would be something I had heard before. I heard Bishop TD Jakes say in one of his old messages, "I know some preachers who can tune, tune, and tune." I knew that at the sound of the organ it was coming. In the midst of all of that, I would find myself sitting in the back or in the choir pondering over the question, "What am I missing God, why what used to work for me no longer works anymore"? Little did I know the answers to my questions had been there the whole time. God was preparing me. God was doing a new thing! What He put in me was something unique and bold. It was also for a specific generation and time. Just as he had instructed Noah, Joseph, and David, it was something entrusted only to me. Sound familiar? <u>Now don't get me wrong, for every chapter in your life, there is something to be learned.</u>

My home church was my first introduction to the word and I was grateful! I have no regrets. The stirring up of the gift started there. It was not a loss but a gain. The Pastor there believed in me. When I announced my calling in 2014, he was the first one to allow me to preach as a guest in his pulpit.

While reading this book I hope you find the strength to hold on to what you have and know that what you have is special.

After finishing this book, my prayer is that you start looking at what you have as something extraordinary and appointed to you by God.

"To be anointed by God means having the favor of God to faithfully do a specific work that HE has chosen you to do in this world" (Bible Study Media, Brooke Holt, 2022). You don't have to be a preacher to be anointed. You can be anointed to do all kinds of things that fulfill the assignments given by God.

Let's take David from the bible for example. David was a shepherd boy called out of the field and anointed by Samuel to be King. God had instructed Samuel to go to the house of Jesse and anoint His next King, but God had not yet told Samuel who it was. When Samuel came to the house, David was not there. He was out tending to the field. Samuel went down the line of all the other brothers in the house, hoping that God would speak and say "this is him", but the oil did not flow. It was only when David showed up the oil was released to flow....whew!!! Glory be to GOD!!

<u>There is an assignment that's held up just for you!!</u> David was accustomed to being out on his own. David was accustomed to being the last one in and not flocking with the others. Does that not say leader? To be a leader, you have to see things in a different light and beyond the now. While David's brothers all ran to feast on today's meal, David was out preparing for the next one! The way he operated spoke anointed. The key qualities of a leader were there from the beginning. When David showed up the oil began to flow. It activated and marked what was already on the inside. God saw what others did not.

<u>What God knows about you is far greater than what others think of you</u>. <u>The dreams and vision He continues to download, pay attention, this is not by happenstance.</u> The word says, "All things work together for the good of those who love God and are called by His purpose." Just like David, there comes a time when you have to come out of the field. God has marked you with a gift and mission that He has watched over for some time now. What is that thing that keeps you up at night? What is that thing that frustrates you? **That could be your call to come out of the field.** God has given us all a unique gift that cannot be erased. As long as you sit on it or run from it....the oil will not flow. Mali said in one of his songs, *"It's you that holds the light, it's not for the taking, remaking or erasing."*

The oil will not flow until you show up. God has chosen you for a certain time, a certain ministry, a certain tribe, and a certain territory. It is time for you to come out of the field and move to the place of promotion, a place of a higher calling. No longer can you apologize for it. Go forth, my friend!! The oil awaits you. If anybody could do it, there would be no reason to anoint. To be anointed also means: to concrete, make sacred, or set apart. You have been chosen, so **STOP APOLOGIZING**!

In the beginning, I asked you, "Are you like me?" If you made it to this point, then it must be that we are alike. Now I want to put the ball back in your court. How many people do you think are out there like you? What God chooses to do through us is never just for us, but for others. There is someone, somewhere, like you blinded and unsure. They are waiting on you. You could very well hold the key to their release.

One of my favorite scriptures is "The Spirit of the Lord is upon me because the Lord has anointed me to bring the Good News to the poor. He has sent me to proclaim that captives will be released, that the blind will see, that the oppressed will be set free" (*English Standard Version*, Luke 4:18).

This scripture speaks to the call that's on your life. It says the Spirit of the Lord is upon who. It's on you and now is your time to own it. Many times we think we are waiting on God, but the majority of the time God is waiting on us.

Now on the flip side of this, there will be those who are not like you and will not like you but guess what?....it's okay. You are not going to be everyone's cup of tea and honestly, that's a good thing. Out of experience, I found that when you strive to meet everyone's expectations you lose your authenticity, become diluted, and get away from what God intended you to be.

If they can define you, they can confine you! Don't do it.

The word says in **John 8:36** that who the Son sets free is free indeed...

The Son paid a price for you to move forward and execute the assignment placed within you.

The Lord says in **John 14:12** that whoever believes in Him will do greater things...

There is a tribe out there for you. I read a quote somewhere one time that said, "Those **who have a problem** with you **don't matter,** and those **who don't have a problem** with you **matter,**" and that's the God-given truth.

Jesus made it clear in His time here on earth who He came for. "I have not come to call the righteous, but to the sinners to repent" (*English Standard Version*, Luke 5:32).

When I read that scripture I can't help but think of the unchurch folk. Jesus was on an assignment for them and understood the assignment. The question now is, will you understand yours?

Jerrika Leakes

Chapter Two

Churching the Unchurched

The Spirit of the Lord is upon me, because he hath anointed me to preach the gospel to the poor; he hath sent me to heal the brokenhearted, to preach deliverance to the captives, and recovering of sight to the blind, to set at liberty them that are bruised, (King James Version, Luke 4:18).

The revelation I received when I first read this scripture was mind-blowing. Isaiah clearly reveals that the assignment on hand is for people with problems. This scripture doesn't speak of those who got it all together, but just the opposite. The people Isaiah talks about in this scripture are the unchurched. They are far from perfect. Let's look at the list:

- The Brokenhearted
- The Poor
- The Confined
- The Blind
- The Bruised

Now if I was to ask you where you can find these people, what would be your response? I'm pretty sure if I was to take a poll on this, most of your answers would be somewhere outside of the structural walls of the church. Many of those who are suffering can't find their way back to the church. It's hard to find something when you have no road map of how to get there, and due to trust issues, many from this list are not willing to stop and ask for directions anymore. I believe this is why God called me to write this book and for such a time as this, I am sounding the alarm to reach the Joshua generation. The Joshua generation are the ones who will come back with a report of hope and belief, instead of a report of too many obstacles. This special task force is made up of the anointed ones who don't mind going into the trenches. They are the Gideon crew. They are the Sauls transformed into Pauls, full of passion but just in need of guidance. The unchurched are no longer breaking the doors down to get into the church. Many of them come from church hurt, so they have migrated to the place of the unknown, and are yearning for revival. The enemy has backed them into the corner of hurt, pain, mistrust, comparison, and disappointment. The enemy thinks he has the one up on this generation, but he is sadly mistaken.

In the famous movie Demolition Man, the main character John Spartan was chosen to go after the most ruthless criminal. They chose him for this impossible mission out of everyone else. John makes a statement in the movie when he is presented with information about his target. He says, "They sent a maniac to catch a maniac." In other words, his opponent had met his match. This is what I feel in the spirit. God has anointed some relentless, non-traditional, go against the grain type of believers to recover the unchurched. God is equipping some faith-filled leaders to church the unchurched. He is sending his demonstration through the ones the others counted out. The word says, "Stop deceiving yourselves. If you think you are wise by this world's standards, you need to become a fool to be truly wise" *(New Living Translation*, 1 Corinthians 3:18). For me, this meant forgetting everything you think you know and trusting what HE said.

When you have a heart for people and want to see everyone win, it just does not sit right with you to see so many stuck in their wilderness. When anointed, it ignites something in you that causes you to rise and take a stance. It takes a genuine and transparent heart to go beyond the walls of shame. "It takes a savage faith" as my friend April Hudson would say. My Pastor always says, "People don't care how much you know until they know how much you care." I don't care how many degrees you have. You can have the alphabet soup behind your name and this upcoming generation still wouldn't care.

Caring is sharing. Just like the motto of St. Louis, this world has become the show me state. If you are not willing to share so that the lost can identify with you then you won't reach them. Nobody wants you to teach them how to battle drug addiction if you have never dealt with addiction. If you have never been married, I don't want you to teach me about marriage or how to keep a husband. Real recognizes real and the truth sets people free. We can't be afraid to share our stories. They used to say back in the day a testimony can preach all by itself. It's time to stop being shameful, stop apologizing for your mishaps, and tell it!! Once you release it, the enemy can no longer hold it over you. No one in this world can say they are perfect. Part of the reason we see so much church hurt and trust issues now is because man allowed people to put them on a pedestal they would never be able to truly stand on.

Now, please understand when I say be transparent that this is not to say be naked. We don't have to conform to the world to connect with the world. Remember what you preach, the practice of that should show. There have to be signs of progression. It's like selling someone a weight loss product and you don't even use it. You've been eating on the word for how long and still no results. You haven't gotten any lighter? My God! In all things make it, make sense. You can't preach prosperity and still walk in poverty. You can't be preaching faith for 10 years and have no evidence. You can't be preaching that you love your spouse and keep having infidelity issues. The enemy can be conning, and what he did, or what we allowed him to do, is to show up in the place where at one time was the safe haven, the church. Accountability got snatched from the church. Man began to seek his own intentions versus God's. Now don't get me wrong, not all churches have fallen short, but there have been enough to allow the devil to make a mockery of us. This was the turning point for me. Listening to God, I understood the assignment in my life would be to break down the wall of man-made religion. I got tired of hearing the way man says to worship God and began to put my ear to the door of Heaven. God said that same gangsta mindset, won't back down attitude, would be the same attributes He would use, but now on His team. Only this time, my "G" mindset would be one of a Glory mindset. I got to the place where I was fed up with seeing my people tricked by the enemy thinking they don't matter and because you don't look like or talk like sister and brother so in so, you don't fit in.

I got tired of hearing women are not supposed to preach, and that if you don't have a theology degree you are not worthy to teach the gospel. In fact, a pastor asked me if I had been to theology school and I replied "No." He then said, "Oh, you are just a preacher on trial." Sir, we all are on trial until Jesus returns. God can use anyone He chooses. God just needs a willing vessel. Will you answer the call? God needs you on His team and for the ones who say otherwise, just tell them, they will know you by your fruit! **Matthew 7:16-18** tells us that a good tree can't produce bad fruit.

Before you move on to the next chapter pray this prayer with me:

Dear Lord,

I thank you for fearfully and wonderfully making me. Thank you that you created me in your own image and likeness. For you are the potter and I am the clay and all things by your hands are perfect. I thank you for each day you have given me. For I know each day you give is a day you call me to walk on purpose. I thank you that you have ordered my steps. Lord as I walk out this journey continue to give me revelation. Help me to keep my eyes on you and ears open to hear what you say. Lord, as I continue to grab a hold of my faith, I ask that you continue to pour out innovative ideas, strategic plans, and visions on how to build your kingdom. Continue to grow me in grace and knowledge through Jesus Christ. To God be all the glory now and forever.

Amen!

Chapter Three

"Benderella"

10 On a Sabbath Jesus was teaching in one of the synagogues, 11 and a woman was there who had been crippled by a spirit for eighteen years. She was bent over and could not straighten up at all. 12 When Jesus saw her, he called her forward and said to her, "Woman, you are set free from your infirmity." 13 Then he put his hands on her, and immediately she straightened up and praised God (New International Version, Luke 13:10-13).

We all are familiar with the story of Cinderella, written by Charles Perrault. Growing up, this was one of my favorite books. Cinderella was a young lady who lived in a home with her stepmother and stepsisters. With a big imagination and big dreams, Cinderella hoped for the opportunity to live a better life. She kept wishing that one day she would find her prince. We all know that her fairy Godmother made it possible for her to experience greatness, but only for a night. Cinderella, excited to go to the ball, in the back of her mind, knew her time would run out by the end of the night. As the clock struck midnight, Cinderella had to flee. If she did not, she risked the chance of her true identity being revealed. Fearful of the thought, she ran. She ran so fast that she lost her slipper. In the end, we know that the shoe she left behind would be the same shoe used to find her again. The determined prince did not give up. He searched all over until she was found. Now I know you are wondering what this has to do with me. Why is she bringing this up? Well, I am so glad you asked. Let me introduce you to Benderella.

Like Cinderella, Benderella had to play the cards she was dealt. Coming from a broken home, like so many others, many times begin with broken pieces. Life starts with an equation and no formula on how to solve it. Why Benderella you may be asking? When all you have is broken pieces, you spend most of your life bending to pick them up. It's hard to walk confidently and keep your head held up when always in a low place. The notion of walking with your head held high is just a mere fairytale. When you can't identify with what you have and don't know your true value, it's easy to bow down to other things. With no fire to ignite purpose, so many times we just settle for whatever. We give into the way of society. We take the Noes and the blows for what they are. Don't get it twisted, I named this character Benderella, but her story is everything but fictional. Instead of standing up for herself, she bowed down. From bad decisions, bad deals, unfortunate circumstances, and bad relationships, Benderella's confidence became low. Taken for granted and misunderstood, it was easier for her just to hide. Benderella was a dreamer who, for so many years, relied on her dreams to keep her going. Could it be that one day there would be a shift in what she saw?

Let me take you to the story of Benderella:

One day Benderella got word of a revival! Now, mind you this invitation came by way of losing a close friend. Pain, fear, restlessness, and bitterness were the vehicle of this revival. Benderella had to get there. Walking into the revival, it was different. There was no choir but someone was playing tracks. This was not an ordinary church. In actuality, the Pastor had just started the church, so at the time he was renting a place to have service. This place was a club on Saturday and a Church on Sunday. She still wonders to this day how that conversation went. How do you ask a club owner to rent his space for church? Looking around she wondered, where are the women in white dresses? No ushers? Where were the organ and piano players? This was not the normal church. This was something different. It was her first time visiting, but she felt like she belonged. With the track bumping in the back, "God is so good", Benderella thought wow, you can actually rap about Jesus. Now mind you, she had been out of church for a long time, but she knew for a fact this was not what she remembered. In observation, the atmosphere felt genuine though. It felt like people actually enjoyed coming to church and not just a routine. This place was lit!! Then it happened. The Pastor got up to deliver the word and it was like He had read Benderella's diary but added JESUS to the mix. That's when it happened. At that moment life stopped. Benderella found her prince. This was no ordinary prince, but one of peace, the Prince of Peace. Through the eyes of Jesus, she found an awakening. The word of Jesus had swept her off her feet. It felt genuine. It felt real!!

Something was still missing from Benderella's journey of healing. She had fallen in love with church all over again, but still would not allow herself to stay long enough for people to know the real her. Let me tell you, persistent Jesus didn't give up on Benderella. He never gave up on her. He waited for her. Two more tragic situations later, she finally surrendered. Benderella came out of hiding. The weight of seeing nothing change in her life became too heavy. The shoe of purpose was hers and it was time to wear it. The same shoe she thought she had lost was the same shoe to her breakthrough!!

Have you ever heard the saying, "If the shoe fits, wear it?" The shoes designed by God fit you and no one else. They are yours. The moment you embrace the real you, a life of freedom and true peace can begin. Yes, for the most part, this story talks about me, but I named it the story of Benderella because I know she symbolically speaks for many. You have been the one always settling, putting everything before you, cleaning up other folks' messes, going through the motions, and never taking time to find out who you truly are or have the potential to be. You are Kingdom!!! You are the child of a King. The crippled woman found in **Luke 13**, had been crippled for eighteen years. My GOD!! It was only when she encountered Jesus, she found peace. She became a product of grace. Benderella learned that we have peace through Jesus Christ. "To know Jesus is to know peace."

Remix!!!... To all my Benderellas, your story is not done. We can't always control what life throws at us, but through the word of God, we can surely find a way to His Kingdom!! Breakthrough can start with just one encounter. If you can just get there and not only get there but find Jesus, He will remember you and He will give you the keys to the Kingdom according to **Matthew 16:19.** Once you receive it guess what? It won't be temporary like Cinderella's night at the ball, but everlasting.

People may have counted you out and said you would never make it, but that doesn't matter because Jesus sees more. **There is a tailor-made shoe that only you can wear.** Truth be told, if you gave others your shoe they probably couldn't even walk in it!! Many can try and put it on, but it won't fit. God made it your shoe for a reason. It's your story and you can have a happy ending if you want it!!! **Stop allowing the devil to capitalize off your story.** Name it and claim it!! The divorce happened, the abuse happened, the letdowns happened, and your past happened, but through it all you made it. Your spoiler alert to the enemy will be, **I may have had to bend, but I did not break! It did not kill me, it built me!!**

Reading this right now should be confirmation that God is trying to get your attention. You matter to Jesus!! **Jeremiah 29:11** says, "For I know the plans and purpose I have for you, declares the Lord. Plans to prosper you and not harm you, plans to give you hope and a future."

Cinderella had glass slippers, but for us, the other Rellas, we walk in bloody shoes I like to call them. With every step, we walk by His grace. We are to walk covered by the blood of Jesus. The shoes fit, so wear them. Rejoice that you've been gifted with them. You may think the clock has stopped, but our thoughts are not like God's thoughts. He sees Kingdom in your life, so walk it out!

Jesus is my Prince of Peace. He met me where I was and brought me into His Kingdom to start living a life of abundance! The revival was the ball I couldn't miss. My recovery, rebirth, and who many know now as Pastor J, came by way of a non-traditional church. It was the encounter with Jesus that changed my life forever, not the structure or look of the building. I now walk with my head held high and happy to name and claim who God called me to be. What will be your story? The first step to finding your fairytale of peace is to first find Jesus. He will give you back the shoe you once lost! I remember many days I would just study and meditate on the book of John. The book of John speaks much about the character and way of life Jesus lived. I recommend it as a starting point for regaining your identity, but let's keep going. In the next chapter, we will look at one of the most common stumbling blocks we trip over and lose our shoes on multiple times.

Pray this prayer with me before we move forward:

Dear Lord,

Thank you for meeting me where I am. There is no place your word can not go. I open up right now to receive your grace. Let your grace flood my heart and mind like never before. I speak peace right now in the name of Jesus. I declare a revival has come and is now here. I declare I won't miss it. This time it will manifest itself. It will not be superficial but supernatural. A divine encounter. For your word says that I am a new creature in Christ, old things have passed away. I am yours oh Lord and you are mine. This means that signs, miracles, and wonders do follow me. Thank you, Lord, for you have kept me all this time. Thank you, Lord, that you never gave up on me and I thank you Lord that you are not even done with me. I Declare that every spiritual blessing you have for my life will be my portion. For you, Lord make every crooked place straight. You Lord have the power to bring every mountain low and every valley high so that I may continue to move forward. It is in you that I live, move, and have my being. I may bend, but I WILL NOT break! No weapon that is formed against me shall prosper. I receive this for myself and everything attached to me, In the name of Jesus.

Amen.

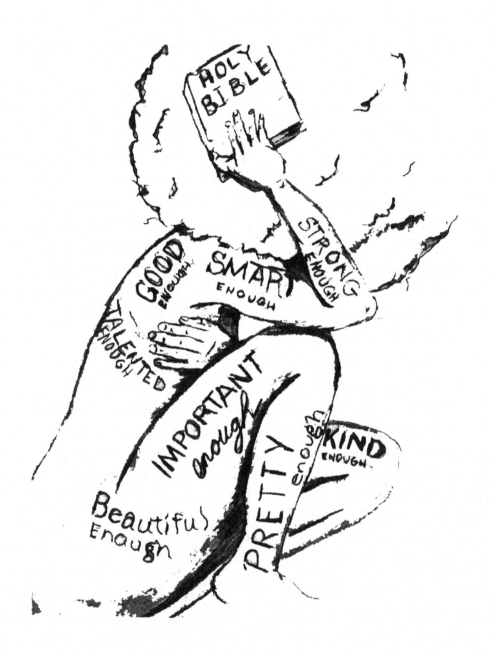

Chapter Four

"They, Them, and The Truth"

But as it is written:
"Eye has not seen, nor ear heard,
Nor have entered into the heart of man
The things which God has prepared for those who love Him"
(1 Corinthians 2:9).

Them, they and the truth, the popular problem, I like to call it. Many people who are anointed have walked away from their assignment because of people. Delays happen because of the opinions of others. Destinations get missed because of others. It's one thing to face adversity because you look at your circumstances, but it's another thing to face adversity because of your circle. When you are anointed, you are also appointed to something. You have to understand that some people are assigned to you and some are not. This was the hardest lesson I had to learn, but when I got it I found freedom.

Let's look at the root of why we care what others think. Many times caring about what other people think is stemmed from the fear of being ridiculed, embarrassed, or people walking away from us. Fear is the derivative of low confidence. We often feel like what we hold is not good enough, so the notion of sharing it with others becomes obsolete. My biggest fear was the thought of what people would think, until one day Jesus met me in the **Book of Mark, Chapters 5:25-34** which reads as follows:

*25 Now a certain woman had a flow of blood for twelve years, 26 **and had suffered many things from many physicians**. She had **spent all that she had and was no better**, but rather grew worse. 27 When she heard about Jesus, she came behind Him in the crowd and touched His garment. 28 For she said, "If only I may touch His clothes, I shall be made well."*

29 Immediately the fountain of her blood was dried up, and she felt in her body that she was healed of the ᵃaffliction. 30 And Jesus, immediately knowing in Himself that power had gone out of Him, turned around in the crowd and said, "Who touched My clothes?"

*31 **But His disciples said to Him, "You see the multitude thronging You, and You say, 'Who touched Me?' "***

*32 And He looked around to see her who had done this thing. 33 But the woman, fearing and trembling, knowing what had happened to her, came and **fell down before Him and told Him the whole truth**. 34 And He said to her, "**Daughter, your faith has made you well**. Go in peace, and be healed of your affliction."*

Now pay attention to the bolded areas, because these are the parts I really want to hone in on, and pray that Holy Spirit speaks to you as He did me. As the preachers say, if I had to put something besides this text, I would tag it, "**What did they give you?**" This is the question God presented me with one morning when reading this scripture. I was in a state of battling with fear and heavy anxiety at the time. I felt the push to start the church but had many debilitating thoughts about what others would think. It paralyzed me. What about the ones who knew me from the club back in the day? What about the crew I used to run with back in the day? What about the ones that knew me as the teen mom back then? What about the ones who say women are not called to preach let alone be Pastors? All these thoughts ran through my head to the point I physically became sick. Then God spoke, "What did **they** give you?" We get so caught up in "they" and "them" that we forget about Him. We forget He holds the truth. My question to you is what has the "they said nation" done for you lately?

Look at the woman with the issue of blood. She had suffered for many years relying on the advice of the physicians. She had invested time and money seeking healing from them, only to pretty much find out she was walking dead. They had no solution to her problem. There was no addition from the "they said nation", only subtraction. She spent all she had and still was no better. Have you ever been there? Many of us with spiritual places of brokenness search high and low to find healing. We attend conferences, we attend women and men empowerment, seek counselors, buy devotions, talk to so-called friends, and still no better than when we came. These things can provide help, but not total healing. That can only come by way of the Word of God and you believing what He says about you. You have to believe and receive it.

Repeat after me, it's an inside job! It was only when the woman with the issue of blood stood up for herself and got to the place where Jesus was, that healing began. She prophesied over herself if I can get to the place of Jesus and touch His hem, I will be made well. **When was the last time you prophesied over yourself?** Has there ever been a first time? Total healing can only come by your declaration and made-up mind. Let me say that again. **Your healing** can only come by **your declaration** and **your made-up mind**.

I have been a registered nurse for several years, and I can tell you, physical healing itself can only come from a made-up mind. The nurses and doctors do well to prepare a plan, but the execution of the plan lies in the hand of the believer. A healthy diet plan can be set for you, but if you choose not to eat means nothing. Physical therapy can be set for you three times a week, but if you choose not to go, strength cannot happen. I say all this to say...they can't do it. Putting your healing completely in their hands won't do it. God has set a plan for you, but if you won't rise up and execute it, healing will not come. God's word says in **Psalms 34:8,** "Taste and see that the Lord is good." In His word, there is a healthy meal plan for you. If you won't eat you will starve! God has a task ahead that will strengthen you, but if you don't go you will never know your full potential.

I remember during my mental battle, I came to a crossroads between what they said and the truth. I remember my heart racing. The heaviness of what people thought of me or what people could do for me, had my feet stuck. It became suffocating. It was either going to be I keep losing my mind or find a way of escape. When I began to call on God that's when He began to call on me. Just like the woman with the issue of blood. She touched Jesus and He knew it. Him knowing it was all that mattered. Where the disciples tried to get Him to overlook it, Jesus could not ignore it. GLORY!! He acknowledged this woman as one of faith because He knew she had been through much trauma, but she did not give up.

He is ready to answer your call. **It wasn't a conference call when He called you.** He wants to meet with you. He wants to talk to you. God is ready to deliver the keys of freedom and purpose to you. People have lived rent-free in your mind for long enough. It's time for you to take back your life. As long as you live on this earth, there will always, always, be someone with something to say. It's the" They said nation", but please know, you don't live there! You live in a place of abundance.

Going back to the question God asked me initially, "What did they give you?" began to hit me. What could man give me that God had not already given me? Nothing! We will talk more about this in the next chapter, but I want to end this chapter with the words Jesus said to the woman. "**Your faith has made you well**. Go in peace, and be healed of your affliction." Receive that today!

Before you move on pray this prayer with me:

Dear Lord,

Help me to take the limits off. I denounce and overthrow every debilitating thing the enemy has tried to mark me with. I break free from the "They said nation." They said I was dead, but I live in the name of Jesus. They said I was sick, but I am healed in the name of Jesus. His word says that by His stripes I am healed. They said I couldn't make it, but God! I have had some major setbacks, but it has positioned me for a major comeback. I am who He says I am. Thank you God that you are not like man. Your love is unconditional. Your love is matchless. I take every negative thought captive to Jesus and declare it is destroyed. Thank you Lord for a new way of thinking. I am a King's Kid. Out of my belly flows rivers of wealth and abundance. I am a Glory Carrier in the name of Jesus! He chose me before the foundations of the world. Eyes have not seen, nor ears heard, nor entered the heart of man, the things God has for me. I have the victory... in Jesus' name

Amen!

Jerrika Leakes

40

Chapter Five

"The Crown or the Sword"

¹⁰ Finally, be strong in the Lord and in his mighty power.¹¹ Put on the full armor of God, so that you can take your stand against the devil's schemes. ¹² For our struggle is not against flesh and blood, but against the rulers, against the authorities, against the powers of this dark world and against the spiritual forces of evil in the heavenly realms. ¹³ Therefore put on the full armor of God, so that when the day of evil comes, you may be able to stand your ground, and after you have done everything, to stand. ¹⁴ Stand firm then, with the belt of truth buckled around your waist, with the breastplate of righteousness in place, ¹⁵ and with your feet fitted with the readiness that comes from the gospel of peace.¹⁶ In addition to all this, take up the shield of faith, with which you can extinguish all the flaming arrows of the evil one. ¹⁷ Take the helmet of salvation and the sword of the Spirit, which is the word of God. (New International Version, Ephesians 6:10-17).

Reading this scripture makes it clear that we are to put on the Full Armor of God. The reason being is that there is a real battle that we face daily. The enemy's attacks and schemes are there to stop God's people from living a life of peace and confidence in His Kingdom. For today's time, it may seem that the enemy is winning and in some cases, he may, but that is because, unlike us, the enemy understands his assignment. He is faithful to his work of trying to kill, steal, and destroy. For us, it becomes complicated. We hesitate, going back and forth in our calling. If

Jerrika Leakes

we are to gain ground, we have to stop wasting time and go forward. **Romans 8:31** tells us "What then shall we say to these things? If God is for me, who can be against me." It's just like we tell our kids, "If you are doing what you are supposed to be doing, I will always back you up". This is what God is telling us. We have backup. When your intentions are pure and your motives are genuine there is no way you can fail. I believe that's why God presented that question to me that I spoke on in chapter four. What can others give you or take from you if you are doing my work? Are we chasing the crown or the sword?

If God called me to a mission, who could stop me or take it away? A title or seat in the pulpit means what? My God sits on the throne all by Himself. I decrease that He may increase according to **John 3:30-35.** Just call me a "John". As much as they come to me, my goal is for them to know HIM. At the end of the day, no one can stop me from giving, serving, blessing, and lifting up the Name of Jesus. **I work from Heaven and not "Applause R US".** Only God can stop the oil from flowing. **If God is in it, then that settles it!** I can preach on a boat, on a goat, or in a moat...why? Because I'm doing it for the right reason. It's not for money, fame, or status, it's for God's Glory. What's your "Why"? Is it for the crown or the sword?

If you've ever watched the movie *Wonder Woman produced by Warner Bros.*, you would notice that Wonder Woman was born into Royalty. She was a princess by way of inheritance, but outside of this, she felt there was more. She was equipped to fight. Wonder Woman loved her home, but looking around and observing the hurt of the people never sat well with her. She felt there was more. Wonder Woman finally made up her mind there was more for her to do outside the walls of her just being the princess. She was purposeful and built to fight. The gifts given were for execution and not for show. She was given the title Wonder Woman, but she was concerned with the Wonder behind the woman. If you notice in the movie many days within the courts of her home the Amazonians practiced and prepared for battle, but it was just practice. There comes a time in your life when you have to move out of the place of practice and into the place of battle. There is a wonder behind the women and men of God. When you know who you are and whose you are, understand there is no need to chase a crown. You already have that. You are a part of a royal priesthood, sons, and daughters of a King. God has given you divine power to take authority and release it here on earth.

What is your focus? Are you keeping the main thing, the main thing? If not, that could be your problem. That could be why your calling and ministry are sucking the life out of you. If it's popularity you seek then I am here to tell you, you will lose every time. Joshua P. Smith said this one time, "If you live for the people's applause then you will die for their rejection." Chasing the crown that people want to give can be an exhausting thing. Just as Jesus was applauded by many He also was left by many, but because He was clear on what His assignment was, He never allowed himself to walk in the realm of trying to be Mr. Popular. If you are not walking in the **truth of your** purpose then you are not living. Just like a product designed by an inventor, made to produce a work, so did God when He made you. Go with that men and women of God!! With the word of God, you will win every time!! You have been given the word as your sword to execute and defeat the enemy. The enemy tries to place fear in your heart to stop you from using your weapon, but it is the weapon that helps us slay! It may seem that the enemy is winning, but as soldiers back in the day would say, "You may have won a battle, but you will not win the war!" The war is already won. The word and promises God has set for you can not be erased. The enemy may have had you down, and you may have lost some things, but if you pick back up the sword which is the word, the devil has no choice but to flee.

You are a Glory kid, adopted into royalty and also called to be a warrior. Effectively, consistently, and strategically speaking God's Word will bring forth a demonstration of His wonder-working power. You have been chosen to show how to get a demon straight! Pick up your sword!!!

Chapter Six

"Lemons into Lemonade"

And we know that all things work together for good to them that love God, to them who are called according to his purpose (*King James Version*, Romans 8:28).

For we know there can be no lemonade without lemons. Lemons are key to making a unique; thirst-quenching drink. It is king to a sweet creation. It is the primary additive needed to even begin. It's kind of like life. Our introduction to the world begins with pain and suffering. Laboring pains give an indication there is a shift in a baby's current place of gestation. From decent to limited room, a baby moves from a place of comfort to the unknown. Life and lessons began. Even as babies we take chances to see if we are capable of doing certain things.

This is the information that many of us understand and grasps with no problem, but the part of the process that we miss is the initial thought of the design, which began with God. **Jeremiah 1:5** says "Before I formed you in the womb I knew you, before you were born I set you apart" (NIV). In the text, God is giving insight to Jeremiah that a plan was there before a physical structure. God had a plan of what He wanted to do on earth and when He would choose to enforce that plan. The outer package came after. The mission met the man/woman and they became one.

How powerful and important does that sound? Exactly! God has a story to tell through you.

You may think the trials and obstacles come to hold you back or take you out, but no, they are there to show your power to overcome. They come so that God can demonstrate through the power of His design. That's you. Like babies learning how to walk, we may stumble and trip up along the way, but it's purposely embedded in our DNA to heal, stand, and walk. You may have lemons that look like limits, but if you change your way of thinking you can very well make lemonade.

My lemons began back when I was just a little girl. I was born with a birth defect. My mom used to wonder why I would bump into things and stumble as a baby. The doctors diagnosed me with a rare eye disease that pretty much declared me legally blind in my right eye at the age of 6. I struggled all through childhood. I was the slowest reader, delayed at finishing things, and later through my young adulthood. I had to fight to get my driver's license. Rejected several times, I finally got the approval, but I would always have restrictions. Lemons!

At the age of 17, I got pregnant right before my senior year with my oldest son. No one in my family had ever been a teen mom. Upon announcement many in my family walked away, doubting that I would ever be successful. Many of my cousins went off to college. I was here with my now husband, baby daddy at the time, raising a baby. Lemons!

Barely passing high school and not making the grades needed to go off to college, I began to walk through my wilderness. Working a dead-end job and unhappy with the choices I had made in life, I coped through distractions. I was clubbing every week, smoking, and drinking. I was searching to fill a void, and at the same time creating a void within my son. Lemons!

After my husband and I got married and we both joined the church was when I reached a turning point, I regained my life. I found a better way of living, but it didn't stop the lemons from piling up. My life was a cycle of check to check, robbing Peter to pay Paul, and having nothing to call my own. The only awakening for me was on Sundays. Being in the place of the word began to stir up gifts. Things that I had dreamed of doing as a little girl started to come up again.

I made up my mind that I wanted to go to nursing school. I believed in myself and believed God's word, but because of my low GPA, I had to start from scratch. I had to take general education classes to even prove that I would be a good candidate for nursing school. What would usually take others 4 years would take me 6 years. I remember saying to myself, "Do I even have the discipline to go to school that long? I didn't have that back in high school." Lemons!

We all have heard the story of how diamonds have to go through fire to be purified. This sounds familiar, but I like the process of making lemonade better. It sits a little closer to home. Diamonds sound good but many have never seen this process firsthand. I think there are many more of you out there who can relate to lemons than diamonds. Many of you have seen the process of making lemonade. Let's go with that. All lemons matter!

In research, I found that for lemon trees to grow and flourish some important things have to take place. The first thing is position. Lemon trees grow best when placed under direct sunlight. If the sun can hit it just right, it grows better. The lemon tree's potential is determined by how well it sits under the sun.

How well do you sit under the Son? Yes, **Son**! Are you always seeking him or are you in and out? Your lemons won't grow that way. In your hands, your lemons look unpromising, but under the Son let me tell you they have potential. **Galatians 2:20** says, "I have been crucified with Christ and I no longer live, but Christ lives in me. The life I now live in the body, I live by faith in the Son of God, who loved me and gave himself for me."

The Son gave his life that I may live. This revelation gave me the understanding that I matter. Even with my lemons, Jesus saw something in me beyond what I could see and said yes. By living by faith and looking at life through the lens of Jesus your lemons can grow. There is nothing too hard for God. Whenever your lemons are under the Son they are clothed with grace and His mercy. When you give it to God and accept Jesus as your Lord and savior, that settles it! Positioned under the Word there is no way you can stay the same.

The next thing we know about making lemonade is that the lemons have to endure much strain to be ready for the next level. Lemon after Lemon we squeeze to obtain enough. Have you obtained enough for the next level?

With all the things life had squeezed out of me, I got to the point I had to do something. It's crazy how the Lord works. He knows that when put in an uncomfortable state we gain haste to make it out. The lemons I had obtained in my life were just lemons until I started to apply pressure.

My delay in obtaining a higher education was a lemon, I knew that I was capable of achieving so much more. With the right touch and strength to pick it up again, I enrolled in school and overcame that obstacle. It took time, and it was hard to push through nursing school but I did it! While in nursing school I became a nurse mentor to those coming in behind me. I applied pressure to my lemons by sharing my story with young women on how if I could do it I know they could. I shared with them how I became positioned under the Son. Many times on test day I would lead the whole class in prayer. After class people would share how much my praying for them helped them through it. God was squeezing me. My lemons were beginning to produce substance. August 10th, 2002 marked the day that I became a teen mom, and coincidentally the same day on August 10th, 14 years later, I graduated with a bachelor's degree in nursing. My son and I took a picture that day. It was a physical birthday for him, but a new birth for me. It's funny how God works. Lemonade!

I believe motherhood and being the oldest child squeezed me to develop the skills of leadership and discipline. In four years, I went from nurse to nurse lead to charge nurse to nurse manager. Something like this doesn't happen every day. Lemonade!

Disclosure: Young girls please do not take this as it's okay to have kids early, that somehow it will make you better. I'm just stating this was my lemon. My lemons don't have to be your lemons.

My husband and I started out young, faced many obstacles, and could have thrown in the towel, but we are still together after all these years. We were junior high-high school sweethearts and held it together with duct tape... lol. In 2010 we rededicated our lives back to Christ and we were baptized together. We came out repositioned under the Son! We've been rocking together ever since. Lemonade!

Never give up on your lemons!! The chapters we create in our life sometimes cause us to take a turn, but the author/editor knows how to bring it all together to make sense in the end. The pressure is a part of the process. It moves you from being stuck to a substance called faith. When all odds are against you, when tired of the cycles, when people continue to take more than they give, you reach the place of faith. Faith will fuel you into a zone where it's go big or go home. Squeezing substance out of lemons can be an ugly not so fun and sometimes messy process but needed to make the lemonade. Many days you may not look like yourself, you may get tired and look worn out, but this is all for the production of your next level! Lemonade!

"Now faith is the substance of things hoped for, the evidence of things not seen" (Hebrews 11:1).

Many of these lemons I picked for myself. They were not the best but they were mine. It was when I studied and unlocked the promises of God I knew I could make more out of them. God had a plan. God had a thought. He purposed that in me and I am grateful. He never gave up on me because he knew what the design was capable of. From labor, decent, place of gestation, pain, and push I was designed and it's in my DNA to rise. I may stumble, I may fall, but I can get up and keep walking every time because of whom I belong to. I don't apologize anymore or hide. I am in the place of the Son Light!

"Life will always bring you lemons, but the lessons will bring you lemonade."

–Pastor J

Chapter Seven

Finally

If you remain in me and my words remain in you, ask whatever you wish, and it will be done for you (New International Version, John 15:7).

"Remember what I told you and you will be fine," were the last words the father in the movie *Hanna* written by Seth Lochhead said to his daughter before the mission. Hanna had been raised in the wilderness by her father since birth. During that time he trained her to be an assassin. He knew that because of who he was they would one day come for her, so he had to prepare her. Living off the grid, Hanna's dad tells her that whenever she is ready for the fight, all she would have to do is hit a button that would raise the signal giving their location. Now, this is important because knowing that her dad had prepared her for the fight, it still would be Hanna's decision to make up her mind when she was ready. One day Hanna opens the case to the button and stares at it. Contemplating whether to hit it or not, she hesitates. She knows that once she hits that button, there is no turning back. Proceeding on, Hanna hits the button and ultimately the enemy comes for her, but what the enemy didn't know is that she was not the average girl. Hanna executed every assignment to ultimately complete her mission, all because her dad had poured everything into her. Whew!

Finally, it's time. In all that we have discussed, you must understand that the time is here and the time is now. Your Dad has trained you for the mission. You may have grown up in the wilderness or even the trenches, but God, your Daddy has prepared you for the fight. You are not an average kid on the block. It may seem like He is not speaking in your life, but it could be that He has spoken, and now waiting on you to decide when to hit the button.

What is your button of purpose?

- The business
- The new career
- The Ministry
- The new relationship
- The calling

What is it? Whatever it is, the enemy is going to attack, that's a given, but that's because of who you are and whose you are. Wherever you find resistance, that's where you will find a hidden treasure. The very thing that you have been running from is the same thing that holds your blessing. This is why it is so important that we always remember the words of our Father. If we can remember the words of Him we will ultimately be able to execute every assignment that is put before us.

It took me years to finally get the place of "Finally Free." This was because I was not confirming and reaffirming what my Daddy said concerning me. People of God, what I found is that the first step to loving yourself and being confident had to come from looking through the lenses of God. My view of all that I had gone through had to be looked at from a different angle. Just as Hanna's father did in the wilderness, I realized God was preparing me the whole time. The things endured were things He knew I could handle. The lessons were the training camp of my faith. Had I not been tried by sickness, I would not be able to appreciate that by His stripes I am healed (Isaiah 53:5). I may live physically blind in one eye, but spiritually I see like an eagle! I once was blind, but now I see (John 9:25). Had I not been faced with the betrayal of people, I would not have understood that He would stick closer than a brother. I can confirm and reaffirm His word that says, "He will never leave me, nor forsake me" in **Deuteronomy 31:6.** The word follows you because you are God's treasure. You are a physical being, but you carry something holy down on the inside of you. God is watching over that thing.

Mark Twain said, **"There are two important days of your life. The day you were born and the day you find out why."**

You were born with reason. You were built not to break but to break through. You were born on purpose.

I finally realized why I had to go through what I went through. I had to struggle and work harder than others because I was called to be a demonstration of His mighty works. I finally understood that God gives His toughest assignments to his toughest warriors. You are called to be a sign, a miracle, and a wonder. The mission given to you is a classified mission. Not all can handle it! God says you can handle it. Many times I have noticed that the times I walked past the place of fear, I found great things and great people. Just look at some examples I have provided.

Faith Walk

1. In 2012, I said "Yes" and became obedient to my calling as an evangelist. The day I preached my first sermon, I had a young lady open up to me and say that my message was her breakthrough. My "Yes" unlocked the door for others to walk through. Faithfully seeking to learn all I could from my leaders and serving, I became the first minister to be ordained by my pastors.

2. In 2015 I chose to walk beyond the place of fear and apply to nursing school. It took me longer than others but as I look back at all that occurred in my life, everything happened at the time it needed to happen. God's timing was perfect! I graduated with my bachelor's and in 4 years became the nurse manager of the outpatient surgery center at the number one trauma center in Memphis, TN.

3. In 2021 again I heard God's voice and was obedient to what He said. I started the church True Revival and Praise Ministries in Memphis, Tennessee during a pandemic. That did not make sense given the state of the world. Churches were closing their doors, but God was calling to open one. Since then many who had not been to church in years have rededicated their life to Christ. Post-pandemic, we are still open. We have virtual (e-members) and physical members.

4. In 2022 I heard God say there was more. I launched my first life coaching business in which God continues to send and produce success. The oil has not stopped yet.

5. On October 24, 2022, I had surgery with complications during my procedure that could have ended my life, but the prayers and faith of my team produced results. God wouldn't allow it. In revelation, I feel God needed me to experience this so that I could obtain another level of faith. Just as he told the enemy concerning Job, "You can test her but you cannot take her life". I am now an on-fire, crazy faith believer in God's word like never before! Mission accomplished.

These are just a few examples of how God has caused things to work in my favor. It would take several books for me to list them all. He has been better than good.

Finally, I understand. No longer do I apologize for who I am and what God has called me to be. My mission is not everyone's mission. I stand now, ready. I stand now hitting the button of purpose. As long as I continue to remember my Father's Word, I know I will be okay. These are the same recommendations I hope you will receive. By God's word, you will be okay. Faith will always create a way. Trust what HIS word says!

Remember the enemy is going to always try to attack. You will always have naysayers, but because God has anointed you there is nothing they can do with you. To stop you would mean the enemy would have to kill you, but he does not have that authority or type of power at all. I heard Evangelist Yvonne Capehart preach one time, "The devil can't kill what God has anointed to live."

You have been anointed to live!!! The enemy has capitalized off your dreams long enough. It's time to break through. Remember your Dad's words and you will be fine!!

Finally, I am done apologizing! Get Ready!!

You made it to the end of this book! I hope this book has blessed you as it has blessed me writing it. I pray that by reading this you have made up your mind to tap into your next level of greatness. When writing this book I knew I wanted it to be seven chapters, because according to my research, the number 7 means completion (Christianity.com, Dolores Smyth, 2020).

In all that's been said within this book, my focus was that you finally get to the place of completion reading the chapters in your life of doubt, fear, and low self-esteem. I stand in agreement with you declaring this is no longer your story. It is finished. Regardless of your disabilities, you have been powered by God to be a light to someone, somewhere. Listed below are affirmations that I want you to confirm and affirm. The way we stay planted, immovable, and in faith is by His word. **1 John 4:4** says "Greater is He that is within you, than you that is in the world".

Jerrika Leakes

Daily Affirmations

This next section includes Affirmations that I have themed for each day of the week to create an area of focus. Each Daily Affirmation is followed by a blank page for you to record your thoughts and reflections for each day.

Monday Manna
Declarations concerning your money and finances

1. For I have something better than money. I have favor with God. Money cannot do what My Father can do! My Father owns everything and what I have HE is able to multiply.

Hebrews 13:5 (ESV). Keep your lives free from the love of money and be content with what you have, because God has said, "Never will I leave you; never will I forsake you."

2. As I anoint my ears for today and open them up to the voice of the Holy Spirit, I am confident that he will give me sound advice, innovative ideas, mind-blowing creativity, and bless my hands to do the work before me.

Deuteronomy 8:18 (ESV). "You shall remember the Lord your God, for it is he who gives you power to get wealth that he may confirm his covenant that he swore to your fathers, as it is this day."

3. God is concerned about everything that concerns me. He is mindful of me. I rejoice in this day that he has made, and rejoice in my tomorrow. God is cooking up something big!

Matthew 6:30 (ESV). "But if God so clothes the grass of the field, which today is alive and tomorrow is thrown into the oven, will he not much more clothe you, O you of little faith?"

4. I will not operate in haste or rush in making bad decisions. I trust God. I stand on HIS word and value His instructions.

Philippians 4:6 (ESV). "Do not be anxious about anything, but in everything by prayer and supplication with thanksgiving let your requests be made known to God."

Matthew 10:30-31 (ESV). "But even the hairs of your head are all numbered. Fear not, therefore; you are of more value than many sparrows."

5. I am the child of a King. I lack nothing.

Philippians 4:19 (ESV). "And my God will supply every need of yours according to his riches in glory in Christ Jesus."

Monday Reflections

_____

_____

_____

_____

_____

_____

_____

_____

_____

_____

_____

_____

_____

_____

_____

Tenacious Tuesday
Motivation to do what you are capable of doing through Christ

1. God has given me dominion. The things around me have to respond to my voice. I speak to every obstacle, hindrance, and barrier in my way and command it to move.

Mark 11:23 (NIV). "Truly I tell you, if anyone says to this mountain, 'Go, throw yourself into the sea,' and does not doubt in their heart *but believes that what they say will happen, it will be done for them."*

2. There is no need for me to fear. My daddy walks and talks with me. He gives me strength. Lord, you said you would help me. Teach me how to speak fluent faith. Give me the words to say to any situation and anyone you bring my way. I am kept by you Oh Lord!

Isaiah 41:10 (NIV). "So do not fear, for I am with you; do not be dismayed, for I am your God. I will strengthen you and help you; I will uphold you with my righteous right hand."

3. Fear is not in my DNA. God gave me a spirit of power, love, and self-control. The enemy cannot and will not move me. The Holy Spirit is my comforter. Faith is my shield! I make Hell nervous. I apply pressure to the enemy's camp.

2 Timothy 1:7 (NKJV). "For God has not given us the spirit of fear but of power, and of love, and of a sound mind.

Joshua 1:9 (NKJV). Have I not commanded you? Be strong and courageous. Do not be afraid; do not be discouraged, for the LORD your God will be with you wherever you go."

4. Even if the day holds trouble, my God will deliver me from it. He never forsakes the righteous. The storms may come but I can withstand them because the lord is my strength to stand. My life will speak of victory and Glorify God.

Psalm 50:15 (ESV). "and call upon me in the day of trouble; I will deliver you, and you shall glorify me."

Psalm 37:25 (NIV). I was young and now I am old, yet I have never seen the righteous forsaken or their children begging bread.

5. I have help today. I always have backup. As I move and effectively operate in my spiritual gifts and Kingdom work, nothing can stop me.

Romans 8:31 (NIV). What, then, shall we say to these things? If God is for us, who can be against us?

6. There is nothing I cannot do. I am capable of obtaining every blessing and being successful in Jesus' Mighty Name.

Philippians 4:13 (NKJV). I can do all things through Christ who strengthens me.

Tuesday Reflections

_____

_____

_____

_____

_____

_____

_____

_____

_____

_____

_____

_____

_____

_____

_____

Wellness Wednesday
Motivation to manage your mind, body, and spirit

1. My heart is the gatekeeper of life. I openly welcome things that are good, positive, pure, and loving. Anything that is not good for me I command it to flee.

Proverbs 17:22 (NLT). A cheerful heart is good medicine, but a broken spirits saps a person's strength.

Philippians 4:8 (NIV). Finally, brothers and sisters, whatever is true, whatever is noble, whatever is right, whatever is pure, whatever is lovely, whatever is admirable—if anything is excellent or praiseworthy—think about such things

2. I denounce the spirit of comparison. I am God's unique design. Fearfully and wonderfully made. Made in His image and in His likeness.

Proverbs 14:30 (NLT). A peaceful heart leads to a healthy body, jealousy is like cancer in the bones.

Psalm 139:14 (NIV). I praise you because I am fearfully and wonderfully made; your works are wonderful, I know that full well.

3. I raise awareness today on what I put into my body. I will not give in to the temptations of the enemy. I tap into my spirit man that will help me to be bold and train for the mission before me. I denounce everything wrapped in my flesh, for it is weak.

1 Corinthians 6:19-20 (NKJV). [19] Or do you not know that your body is a temple of the Holy Spirit who is in you, whom you have from God, and that you are not your own? [20] For you were bought at a price: therefore glorify God in your body and in your spirit which are God's.

Matthew 26:41 (KJV). Watch and pray, that ye enter not into temptation; the spirit indeed is willing, but the flesh is weak.

Romans 12:1-2 (NLT). And so, dear brothers and sisters, I plead with you to give your bodies to God because of all he has done for you. Let them be a living and holy sacrifice—the kind he will find acceptable. This is truly the way to worship him. 2 Don't copy the behavior and customs of this world, but let God transform you into a new person by changing the way you think. Then you will learn to know God's will for you, which is good and pleasing and perfect.

4. I direct my focus to the plans and purpose God has set before me. I have a direct line of communication to the Lord. I do not look at what's in front of me(obstacles, lack, or pain) but I look at what's ahead of me. God tells me that the plans He has for me are good and not for evil.

Jeremiah 29:11 (NIV). For I know the plans I have for you," declares the LORD, "plans to prosper you and not to harm you, plans to give you hope and a future.

Colossians 3:2 (ESV). *Set your minds on things that are above, not on things that are on earth.*

Jerrika Leakes

Wednesday Reflections

_____

_____

_____

_____

_____

_____

_____

_____

_____

_____

_____

_____

_____

_____

Thankful Thursday
Thanking God for all He has done

1. This is the day that the Lord has made. I will rejoice and be glad on this day. I thank you Father for ordaining this day, blessing this day, and carrying me through this day!

Psalm 118:24 (NIV). The LORD has done it this very day; let us rejoice today and be glad.

Genesis 1:27-28 (KJV). ²⁷ *So God created man in His own image, in the image of God He created him; male and female he created them.* ²⁸ ***God blessed them***; *and God said to them, "Be fruitful and multiply, fill the earth, and subdue it; have dominion over the fish of the sea, over the birds of the air and over every living thing that moves on the earth."*

2. As I look over my home and all that is connected to me, I give thanks to you God that all is well. I am sure of it!

Philippians 1:6 (ESV). And I am sure of this, that he who began a good work in you will bring it to completion at the day of Jesus Christ.

3. Thank you God that you chose me. Thank you God that you never give up on me. Thank you God for being patient with me.

John 15:16 (NKJV). You did not choose me, but I chose you and appointed you that you should go and bear fruit and that your fruit should remain, that whatever you ask the Father in My name, He may give you.

Ephesians 1:4 (NIV). For he chose us in him before the creation of the world to be holy and blameless in his sight. In love.

4. Thank you God that you have given me the fruit of every spiritual blessing. Thank you that I have access to an open heaven.

Ephesians 1:3 (ESV). Blessed be the God and Father of our Lord Jesus Christ, who has blessed us in Christ with every spiritual blessing in the heavenly places.

5. Thank you for being a healer!

Isaiah 53:5 (NKJV). But He *was* wounded for our transgressions, *He was* bruised for our iniquities; the chastisement for our peace *was* upon Him, And by His stripes we are healed.

6. Thank you God you are a provider!

Philippians 4:19 (NKJV). And my God shall supply all your needs according to His riches in glory by Christ Jesus.

7. Thank you God you are my protector!

2 Samuel 22:3-4 (NIV). 3 The Lord is my rock, my fortress and my deliverer; my God is my rock, in whom I take refuge, my shield and the horn of my salvation. He is my stronghold, my refuge and my savior– from violent people you save me. 4 I called to the Lord, who is worthy of praise and have been saved from my enemies.

8. Thank you God you are a deliverer! You hear my voice. You know my cry. What concerns me concerns you. Thank you for saving me and never letting me fall. My life will glorify you! In Jesus' Mighty Name!

Psalm 50:15 (ESV). and call upon me in the day of trouble; I will deliver you, and you shall glorify me.

Psalm 107:6 (NIV). *Then they cried to the Lord in their trouble, and he delivered them from their distress.*

Thursday Reflections

_____

_____

_____

_____

_____

_____

_____

_____

_____

_____

_____

_____

_____

_____

_____

Faith Filled Friday
Declarations to catapult you into your next level

1. I am more than a conqueror. I was created for great things and to be a light in dark places.

Romans 8:37 (ESV). No, in all these things we are more than conquerors through him who loved us.

Genesis 1:26 (ESV). Then God said, "Let us make man in our image, after our likeness. And let them have dominion over the fish of the sea and over the birds of the heavens and over the livestock and over all the earth and over every creeping thing that creeps on the earth."

John 8:12 (NKJV). "Then Jesus spoke to them again, saying, 'I am the light of the world. He who follows Me shall not walk in darkness, but have the light of life.'"

John 14:12 (NIV). Very truly I tell you, whoever believes in me will do the works I have been doing, and they will do even greater things than these, because I am going to the Father.

2. My faith is the key to my breakthrough. I face it and embrace it today. Regardless of what it looks like I will keep going because, in the end, it will speak of victory. No one or nothing can tell me differently. I am not a spectator but a demonstrator of God's work.

Hebrews 11:1 (NKJV). Now faith is the substance of things hoped for, the evidence of things not seen.

Hebrews 11:6 (ESV). And without faith it is impossible to please him, for whoever would draw near to God must believe that he exists and that he rewards those who seek him.

1 Corinthians 2:9 (NKJV). But as it is written: "Eye has not seen, nor ear heard, Nor have entered into the heart of man The things which God has prepared for those who love Him."

3. Men may say it can't be done, but I know differently. My daddy can do all things but fail.

Matthew 19:26 (NIV). Jesus looked at them and said, "With man this is impossible, but with God all things are possible."

4. My Faith is connected to the mouth of the Holy Spirit. My ears hear His voice and every other voice is a stranger to me.

Romans 10:17 (ESV). So faith comes from hearing, and hearing through the word of Christ.

John 10:5 (NIV). But they will never follow a stranger; in fact, they will run away from him because they do not recognize a stranger's voice."

5. My faith is my superpower. I see double. I see beyond what's in front of me. Faith will show me the way and lead me to victory.

2 Corinthians 5:7 (NKJV). For we walk by faith, not by sight.

6. The enemy may have weapons, but they are no match for my faith. I break through and destroy every trap the enemy has set.

Ephesians 6:16 (ESV). In all circumstances take up the shield of faith, with which you can extinguish all the flaming darts of the evil one.

Isaiah 54:17 (NKJV). No weapon formed against you shall prosper, and every tongue which rises against you in judgment You shall condemn. This is the heritage of the servants of the Lord, and their righteousness is from Me," Says the Lord

7. There is abundant power flowing within me. As I tap into it, God will release record-breaking results, mind-blowing results, miracle after miracle, and favor beyond what I can phantom.

Ephesians 3:20 (ESV). *Now to him who is able to do far more abundantly than all that we ask or think, according to the power at work within us.*

Friday Reflections

_____

_____

_____

_____

_____

_____

_____

_____

_____

_____

_____

_____

_____

_____

_____

_____

_____

Saturday Soak
Confirmation of who you are and whose you are

Affirmation	Reference Verse
1. I am the child of the King.	Ephesians 1:11
2. I am rooted and grounded in love.	Ephesians 3:17
3. I make hell nervous	
4. I am blessed with all spiritual blessings in heavenly places in Christ Jesus.	Ephesians 1:3
5. I command the morning of this day and speak life over everything attached to me. Life and death are in the power of my tongue.	Proverbs 18:21 Ephesians 4:22–23
6. Today is a new day. My mind is renewed.	Revelations 12:11
7. I am an overcomer	Ephesians 2:5
8. I am saved by His grace	Ephesians 2:10
9. I am Your workmanship	Ephesians 1:4
10. I am anointed and appointed	Luke 4:18
11. God loves me always!	John 3:16

Saturday Reflections

_____

_____

_____

_____

_____

_____

_____

_____

_____

_____

_____

_____

_____

_____

_____

_____

Sunday Sizzle
Find a church home where you can grow, be strengthened in the word, and help continue building God's Kingdom

Letter to the Unchurched and Prophetic Message:

Dear Friend,

I know some of you have been hurt, rejected, and neglected. My heart goes out to you for I understand what it feels like to deal with this kind of pain. However, it was never God's intent for you to live in silos. God called us to work together. Right now where you are, you must forgive. Yes, the offenses did happen, but it is not your end. It's time to live again. It's time to be born again. The Kingdom of God needs you. My prayer for you is that God increases your discernment to find the church where you can be blessed and filled. There are so many good churches and true men and women of God out there. You could be the hold-up for others around you. It's time to get back on your post. You have so many gifts lying dormant. They say the grave is the richest place in the world because so many die with incomplete missions. Do not let the enemy continue to capitalize on your dreams and goals. The Kingdom needs you. I need you! Together we can stand against anything. Together we can build bridges and heal our land. With all of our creative gifts, we can move mountains.

Love,

Jerrika Leakes

Sunday Reflections

_____

_____

_____

_____

_____

_____

_____

_____

_____

_____

_____

_____

_____

_____

_____

_____

_____

Reflection Wrap-Up

_____

_____

_____

_____

_____

_____

_____

_____

_____

_____

_____

_____

_____

_____

_____

_____

Bag Secured!